INDEPENDENT
THINKING
ON ...

C000183257

LOSS

Ian Gilbert
with William, Olivia and Phoebe Gilbert

A LITTLE BOOK ABOUT BEREAVEMENT FOR SCHOOLS

ındependent
thinking press

First published by

Independent Thinking Press
Crown Buildings, Bancyfelin, Carmarthen, Wales, SA33 5ND, UK
www.independentthinkingpress.com

and

Independent Thinking Press
PO Box 2223, Williston, VT 05495, USA
www.crownhousepublishing.com

Independent Thinking Press is an imprint of Crown House Publishing Ltd.

© Ian Gilbert, William Gilbert, Olivia Gilbert, Phoebe Gilbert
and Crown House Publishing, 2020.

The rights of Ian Gilbert, William Gilbert, Olivia Gilbert and Phoebe Gilbert to be
identified as the authors of this work have been asserted by them in
accordance with the Copyright, Designs and Patents Act 1988.

First published 2020.

All rights reserved. Except as permitted under current legislation no part of this work may be
photocopied, stored in a retrieval system, published, performed in public, adapted, broadcast,
transmitted, recorded or reproduced in any form or by any means, without the prior permission
of the copyright owners. Enquiries should be addressed to
Independent Thinking Press.

Independent Thinking Press has no responsibility for the persistence or accuracy of URLs for
external or third-party websites referred to in this publication, and does not guarantee that any
content on such websites is, or will remain, accurate or appropriate.

Quotes from Ofsted and Department for Education documents used in this publication have
been approved under an Open Government Licence. Please see: http://www.nationalarchives.
gov.uk/doc/open-government-licence/version/3/.

Pages 12–13: extract from E. De, *Research Network on Severe and Multiple Disadvantage: A
Literature Review Into the Prevalence and Impact of Loss and Bereavement on Individuals
Experiencing Severe and Multiple Disadvantage* (December 2018), pp. 6–7. Available at: http://
www.revolving-doors.org.uk/file/2331/download?token=K316AqwO.

The Independent Thinking On ... series is typeset in Azote, Buckwheat TC Sans,
Cormorant Garamond and Montserrat.

The Independent Thinking On ... series cover style was designed by Tania Willis
www.taniawillis.com.

British Library Cataloguing-in-Publication Data
A catalogue entry for this book is available from the British Library.

Print ISBN 978-178135353-0
Mobi ISBN 978-178135363-9
ePub ISBN 978-178135364-6
ePDF ISBN 978-178135365-3

LCCN 2020930029

Printed and bound in the UK by
Gomer Press, Llandysul, Ceredigion

For Grandad.

'When a person we love so much leaves us, it is hard, but we draw strength from the life they lived, from the memories they have left us and from the hope that they held for the lives we have left to live.'

FOREWORD

Since establishing Independent Thinking in 1994, we have worked hard to share with educators around the world our belief that there is always another way. The Independent Thinking On ... series of books is an extension of that work, giving a space for great educators to use their words and share great practice across a number of critical and relevant areas of education.

Independent Thinking on Loss is a welcome but challenging addition to this series, looking not so much at the nature of teaching and learning or the wider education system but, instead, at what a school can do when the worst happens to a child in it. As it will.

Nothing prepares us for the loss of a loved one, regardless of our age. Or theirs. Whether we know that death is imminent, expected and inevitable or whether someone is snatched away from us so suddenly that we never had time to say goodbye, neither is better, neither is right; whatever happens, the loss hits us and it really, really hurts.

As part of our duty of care to the children and young people in our classrooms, the least we can do is to prepare ourselves to deal with a child losing a loved one. This is important not only because we can help to minimise the disruption to their schooling and their future lives, but also because it's the right thing to do.

But what do you do when you are faced with the situation of a child losing someone close to them and you simply don't know what you should say or not say, do or not do?

This book will help you to answer that question.

The memory of June 2008 is forever etched on the lives of Ian Gilbert (founder of Independent Thinking) and his three amazing children, William, Olivia and Phoebe. Their hopelessness and anger, courage and bravery after the children lost their mum comes through loud and clear in this hard-hitting book. Many people around them at the time did the right thing. Many did the wrong thing. Worse, many did nothing.

The overwhelming need for schools and communities to at least have an idea of what to do in order to help children who are experiencing loss, and its aftermath, is why this book is so important.

NINA JACKSON
CRAIG CEFN PARC

CONTENTS

Foreword .... *i*

I.   Fergus Crow, CEO, Winston's Wish 1

II.   Ian Gilbert, Founder, Independent Thinking 5

III. William Gilbert, Customer Experience Manager,
     Dubai 25

IV. Olivia Gilbert, Lending Associate, Melbourne 31

V.   Phoebe Gilbert, Final Year Student, Sheffield 37

VI. The Lessons 43

    One 45

As soon as the death is known to the school, have a senior member of staff talk to the immediate classmates about what has happened. Stamp out any gossip and offer support for those who may be affected.

    Two 47

Send a condolence card and encourage classmates to do the same. Saying 'I didn't know what to do' and doing nothing is a form of moral cowardice – and why should you be let off the hook? No one else knows what to do either.

    Three 50

When the child comes back to school talk to them (but don't patronise them). Ask them how they would like their teachers to act.

    Four 53

Teach other children to know what to say and how to handle things.

Five 55

School can be the place to escape from what is going on at home ('Home is home and school is school'). Respect that wish as much as possible.

Six 57

Grieving is mentally and physically exhausting.

Seven 59

Be tolerant of homework and other work commitments – evenings may well be spent grieving and talking, not working. Agree work commitments with the child, though, and be firm but caring as you try to ensure they don't get too far behind (and thereby add a feeling of failure to their grieving).

Eight 61

Talk to the spouse if they come to the school. Show them you know and care and are there to help. Don't just ignore them because you don't know what to say. That is more moral cowardice.

Nine 64

Keep on talking to the child and letting them know you still remember, even just in small ways.

Ten 66

Remember the anniversaries.

Eleven 69

Be aware of areas you may cover in the curriculum that may bring back memories (Mother's Day, Father's Day, birthdays, life after death in RE, areas that touch on any illness such as cancer or mental illness and so on).

Twelve 71

When another parent dies, make sure you are mindful of other children who have lost parents, or

CONTENTS

indeed any loved one, as it will bring many memories back.

Thirteen 73
Learn about helping children to cope with bereavement from the various agencies out there.

Fourteen 76
Time heals in bereavement as much as it does following an amputation. It is just what you go through to come to terms with things better.

Fifteen 78
Thank you for taking the time to read this. You can make a terrible situation a bit less stressful for a grieving family.

VII. Resources 79

Let's not tell our sad stories.

JERRY MAGUIRE (1996)

I

FERGUS

This is a unique and special book.

Schools need practical, everyday guidance on how to support bereaved children in schools. But they also need to hear and feel how children and young people experience this support, to tune into what are so often unheard voices, to truly understand what they need and what they want.

Around 45,000 children and young people in the UK experience the bereavement of a parent or a sibling every year.[1] It is a significant number, and the effects can be devastating. At the very least, that is around one child in every classroom in this country.

We know that teachers want to help, that grief and bereavement feel real to them, and that they can make a difference in how a grieving child or young person journeys through their grief over time. But we also know that teachers don't always know what to do and worry that they don't have the skills to talk to grieving children. Most people (teachers included) worry that they will make it worse, not better.

Like everything in teaching, it is both a huge responsibility and a real opportunity.

I don't know of anything else that manages to combine the practical knowledge that teachers need with personal wisdom, drawn from the profound and real experiences of sorrow and loss. What Ian, William, Olivia and Phoebe have done is to give voice to the reality of grief in a family, and to the experience of being bereaved children and young people negotiating the everyday reality of life in school.

Their response is optimism, and this book is imbued with the hope that, in sharing what they know and have

1   See https://schoolsweek.co.uk/child-bereavement-plans-schools/.

experienced, more schools will be able to help more children and young people through their loss.

If anything can help to change the acoustics in schools for grieving children and young people, this book can.

FERGUS CROW, CEO, WINSTON'S WISH

II
IAN

In 2008 my wife died. It was terrible. It was unexpected. In its own awful way, it was a relief. Mental illness brings with it to family life an inner chaos that radiates turmoil. Tragically, it also eats away at childhoods. At the time of the accident, our three children had already been through a great deal. Phoebe was nine when her mother died. Olivia was thirteen. The last time William saw his mother was on his eighteenth birthday, five days before she died.

Several months after their mother's death, BBC's *Newsround* aired a brave and, at the time, controversial programme in which four children talked about their own experiences of losing a loved one.[1] This prompted us to sit down and think about how we could use the network of Independent Thinking schools to get across to teachers what they could do to help children who have lost a parent or a close loved one based simply on our own experiences. To begin with, we did this by way of a fifteen-point PDF handout on one side of A4. Our points were so welcomed by teachers that we decided to elaborate upon them for schools everywhere. What grew out of that work was *The Little Book of Bereavement for Schools*,[2] and this book, *Independent Thinking on Loss*, is the latest iteration of that original and highly regarded work.

In this way we can not only ensure that a whole new generation of teachers will get the messages we believe are so important, but we can also update the reader on how things are still unfolding, even now, a decade and more later.

As for the circumstances of how my children lost their mother, I am pleased to say that over the last ten years

---

1 Gone: Newsround Special Programme on Coping with Death, *Newsround*, BBC One (4 August 2011). Available at: https://www.bbc.co.uk/newsround/14394831.

2 I. Gilbert, W. Gilbert, O. Gilbert and P. Gilbert, *The Little Book of Bereavement for Schools* (Carmarthen: Crown House Publishing, 2010).

mental illness has all but lost the taboo it had back then. Denial kills, after all. I am no royalist, but the manner in which princes William and Harry have spoken about losing their mother and raised awareness of a range of emotional health issues has helped significantly. If the royals are talking about it, then it will be in *The Telegraph,* which means those most embarrassed by such an illness may have to admit that it exists.

In our experience.

But our experience was what *The Little Book of Bereavement for Schools* was all about. Simply the four of us describing in all honesty the personal experiences we had and what, perhaps, primary schools, secondary schools and sixth form colleges could (a) do more of, (b) do differently and (c) never do again to help all those other children and young people who will experience loss too.

And they will experience it.

According to a report by the Childhood Bereavement Network, 41,000 children in the UK lost a parent in 2015.[3] Or, to put it another way, that is one parental death every twenty-two minutes, statistically speaking. If you haven't experienced such tragedy in your school yet, you will. It's just a question of time. With that in mind, what are you going to do to be ready for it? Or will your response be like the following, as one teacher at a bereavement conference that the girls and I were addressing a few years ago described it?

A child lost a parent. We didn't know what to do, so we did nothing. Then things moved on. Then it

---

3 See http://www.childhoodbereavementnetwork.org.uk/research/key-statistics.aspx.

happened it again. And we still didn't know what to do, so we did nothing again.

Of course, schools are busy places and teachers are busy people. There are limits to what they can achieve with so much to teach, so many to teach it to and so little time to fit it all in. Not to mention their own natural and cultural squeamishness and clumsiness in talking about death. As a society, it is one taboo too far, so we tend to avoid it. Although maybe there are changes ahead. According to a recent special issue of *New Scientist* magazine bearing the headline 'The Way We Die Now',[4] there is at least one 'death café' in London where you can enjoy tea and cake while exploring questions such as, 'If you planted an apple tree in the ground where your mum had been composted, would you then eat the apples?'[5]

And, of course, teachers are human too. They have their own sad stories and like attending weddings and watching *Love Actually*, we are all susceptible to the triggers that bring vivid memories and strong emotions rushing back in a way we can never control.

Nor should we try to. 'Better out than in' has been a family motto of ours for quite a while now.

All of which means that the question of whether schools feel it is their place to address issues of bereavement and loss head-on depends on their understanding not only of their role but also of the link between childhood bereavement, well-being and academic achievement.

---

4   *New Scientist*, Issue 3257 (23 November 2019). Available at: https://www.newscientist.com/issue/3257.

5   For more such questions to help open up conversations around death and loss, check out the Thunks on Death resource on the Winston's Wish website at: https://www.winstonswish.org/wp-content/uploads/2019/06/Winstons-Wish-thunks.pdf.

Let's address the last point straight away. Put simply, emotionally balanced children do better in their exams. Duh! Research from Southampton University for Public Health England in 2014 described the effect on academic attainment that schools can enjoy when emotional health and well-being is high on their list of priorities:

1   *Pupils with better health and wellbeing are likely to achieve better academically.*

2   *Effective social and emotional competencies are associated with greater health and wellbeing, and better achievement.*

3   *The culture, ethos and environment of a school influences the health and wellbeing of pupils and their readiness to learn.*

4   *A positive association exists between academic attainment and physical activity levels of pupils.*[6]

Despite Teflon-coated schools ministers dismissing as 'ghastly' initiatives such as social and emotional aspects of learning[7] – even though actual experts, such as Independent Thinking's resident paediatric neurologist Dr Andrew Curran, can see the value in it: Andrew told me that he personally viewed it as the most important innovation to hit primary education for forty years – we can see a clear link between happy and healthy children and academically successful schools.

---

6   F. Brooks, *The Link Between Pupil Health and Wellbeing and Attainment: Briefing for Head Teachers, Governors and Staff in Education Settings* (London: Public Health England, 2014), p. 4. Available at: https://assets.publishing.service.gov. uk/government/uploads/system/uploads/attachment_data/file/370686/HT_ briefing_layoutvFINALvii.pdf.

7   Daily Mirror, Kids To Be Taught Respect (30 April 2007). Available at: https:// www.mirror.co.uk/news/uk-news/kids-to-be-taught-respect-470934.

What, then, of the link between bereavement and well-being? This is where it gets complicated.

The worst has happened. You've sent some cards (hopefully), you've been to the funeral (probably), you're doing your best to make sure the bereaved child gets on with school like any other child and, of course, life goes on (usually).

Again, let's look at the research, of which there is not a great deal, but it is a growing area, I'm pleased to say. Like anything to do with human existence, and especially where that intersects with education, it's complicated. The headlines are all too stark though. A seminal research project interrogated the data from the 1970 British Cohort Study into family life and outcomes. It identified a range of outcomes including:

Children in bereaved [...] families were both more likely to leave full-time education at age 16, and less likely to go on to attain any qualifications at age 16.

Children in bereaved [...] families were also more likely to express lower educational aspirations for the future.

Children who had experienced a parental bereavement [...] were the most likely to show symptoms of depression at age 16.

Lower percentages of men from bereaved [...] families reported being in full-time employment at the age 30 BCS70 interview.

Men from bereaved and disrupted families were more likely than those from intact families to be unemployed or permanently sick at the age 30 BSC70 interview.

A higher proportion of men from bereaved families [...] were in partly skilled or unskilled manual work.

Higher proportions of men from bereaved [...] families report their general health as 'fair' or 'poor' compared with men from intact families.

One quarter of women from bereaved families [...] reported feeling that they 'never seem to get what they want out of life'.

Women from bereaved [...] families reported a high number of symptoms associated with depression compared with [...] women from intact families.[8]

And there's more. According to a trawl of the literature on behalf of the Research Network on Severe and Multiple Disadvantage:

Children who have suffered significant losses will be more likely to offend in adolescence than children for whom there is no evidence of loss.

Those who experienced the death of a parent during childhood have a greater risk of violent criminal convictions [...] and increased risk of somatic symptoms, accidents and mortality, with bereaved children 50% more likely to die before middle age than those not bereaved.

[There is an] increased likelihood that [bereaved children] will partake in risky health behaviours, with higher rates of substance and alcohol use and early pregnancy.

[T]hose who experience the suicide of a parent during their childhood or adolescence are 3 times more likely than non-bereaved peers to themselves die by suicide and those who experienced the accidental death of a parent as a child are 2

---

8   S. Parsons, Long-Term Impact of Childhood Bereavement: Preliminary Analysis of the 1970 British Cohort Study (BCS70). CWRC Working Paper (September 2011), pp. 7–10. Available at: https://assets.publishing.service.gov.uk/ government/uploads/system/uploads/attachment_data/file/181353/ CWRC-00081-2011.pdf.

times as likely to die by suicide. [...] Both groups have a greater risk of hospitalisation for all types of psychiatric disorder compared to the non-bereaved population.

Around 1/3 of bereaved children reach clinical levels of behavioural or emotional difficulty during the two years following a parent's death.

[T]here is evidence that young people with a range of mental health difficulties are more likely to have experienced the death of parent than those with no such disorders.

Bereaved people make greater use of healthcare services [...] including GP services, mental health services, acute and psychiatric hospitals, and consumption of medicines.

Traumatic loss may prompt the bereaved to turn to substance abuse.

[And] a number of studies have found that loss is linked to alcoholism – either its initiation or its increase.[9]

And then there's prison:

Young people involved in offending experience parental, multiple and traumatic deaths at a higher frequency than in the general population.[10]

Not to mention many reports, including one from Public Health England, which highlights bereavement as a potential cause of homelessness.[11]

---

9 E. De, *Research Network on Severe and Multiple Disadvantage: A Literature Review Into the Prevalence and Impact of Loss and Bereavement on Individuals Experiencing Severe and Multiple Disadvantage* (December 2018), pp. 6-7. Available at: http://www.revolving-doors.org.uk/file/2331/download?token=K316AqwO.

10 N. Vaswani, Bereavement Among Young Men in Prison, *Criminal Justice Matters* 98 (17 November 2014). Available at: https://www.crimeandjustice.org.uk/publications/cjm/article/bereavement-among-young-men-prison.

11 Public Health England, Homelessness: Applying All Our Health (2 November 2018). Available at: https://www.gov.uk/government/publications/homelessness-applying-all-our-health/homelessness-applying-all-our-health.

The first time I came across statistics and research such as this was at the conference I mentioned before. I had offered to speak, and my two girls were keen to contribute in their own way too. We were all rather taken aback by these figures. My children's experiences both prior to and as a result of the death of their mother meant that they were definitely prime candidates to be well and truly off the rails. But they weren't.

They were hurting but they were intact, just about.

In fact, this is one of the problems with matching the research to the reality, and it is also one of the issues facing the work on adverse childhood experiences (ACEs) which many in education are currently exploring. The ACEs focus grew out of the work of controversial US private healthcare company Kaiser Permanente's work on obesity in the 1990s.[12] They unexpectedly discovered a link between patients who dropped out of obesity control programmes and the sexual abuse that these patients had experienced during childhood. The initial research entailed a question-naire being sent to 13,494 patients, of which 9,508 responded, which sought to ascertain if they had experi-enced any of the following adverse experiences during childhood:

● Psychological abuse.

● Physical abuse.

● Sexual abuse.

● Violence against their mother.

● Substance abuse by a member of the household.

● Mental illness in a member of the household.

---

12 See https://en.wikipedia.org/wiki/Kaiser_Permanente#Controversies.

● Criminal behaviour leading to jail time by any member of the household.

They then not only looked for links between experiencing one of the above and later negative health outcomes, but also, importantly, the effects of one *or more* of these diverse experiences by way of a grading system (one ACE received a grade of 1, two ACEs a grade of 2 and so on). What they found was 'a strong dose response relationship between the breadth of exposure to abuse or household dysfunction during childhood and multiple risk factors for several of the leading causes of death in adults'.[13]

While this research has attracted worldwide attention for all the right reasons, it has also been called into question, not least by a House of Commons Science and Technology Select Committee paper on early years intervention which advocated a more cautious approach to its findings. Agreeing that the ACEs research and subsequent 'framework' has been useful in raising awareness of such issues and has given practitioners a common language in this area, the committee also highlighted concerns among the scientific community regarding the old scientific nutmeg of mistaking correlation for causation, suggesting that 'the simplicity of this framework and the non-deterministic impact of ACEs mean that it should not be used to guide the support offered to specific individuals'.[14]

One group of academics, headed by Dr Jen Macvarish of the University of Kent, contributed to the select

---

13 V. J. Felitti, R. F. Anda, D. Nordenberg, D. F. Williamson, A. M. Spitz, V. Edwards, M. P. Koss and J. S. Marks, Relationship of Childhood Abuse and Household Dysfunction to Many of the Leading Causes of Death in Adults, *American Journal of Preventive Medicine* 14(4) (1998): 245-258 at 251.

14 Science and Technology Select Committee, *Evidence-Based Early Years Intervention*, 14 November 2018, HC 506 2019-2019, para. 17. Available at: https://publications.parliament.uk/pa/cm201719/cmselect/cmsctech/506/50605.htm.

committee's findings, and were particularly circumspect about the ACEs research, highlighting that the work was 'the latest in a long line of diagnoses of, and simple solutions to, complex social issues in the search for interventions that "work"'.[15] Citing concerns around the need to 'distinguish between science and scientism' they conclude their evidence to the select committee with the following statement:

> *We would argue that the campaign encouraging teachers, health and social care professionals to be 'ACEs-aware' should be subject to serious questioning. While, of course, they should be looking out sympathetically and proactively for the children in their care, this is very different from performing amateur diagnoses of children as having high or low ACE scores. The further rolling out of the ACEs approach would be a very dangerous way to proceed.*[16]

In other words, it's complicated.

Regardless of the fact that the loss of a parent does not even make it on to the ACEs list, personal experience shows us that statistics and real human beings are two different beasts, and just because the numbers indicate you should doesn't mean to say you will.

Like being made redundant or watching *Love Actually*, we all respond in different ways, and how we respond has a great deal to do with what was happening prior to the traumatic event and who is around us as we go through it. This is why the research from the University of Cambridge

---

15 R. Edwards, V. Gillies, E. Lee, J. Macvarish, S. White and D. Wastell, The Problem with 'ACEs'. EY10039: Edwards et al.'s Submission to the House of Commons Science and Technology Select Committee Inquiry into the Evidence-Base for Early Years Intervention (12 December 2017), p. 1. Available at: https://blogs.kent.ac.uk/parentingculturestudies/files/2018/01/The-Problem-with-ACEs-EY10039-Edwards-et-al.-2017-1.pdf.

16 Edwards et al., The Problem with 'ACEs', p. 7.

that leading UK childhood bereavement charity Winston's Wish commissioned in 2019 makes for very interesting – and more nuanced – reading.[17]

Drawing on the best and latest (and some of that was from the 1960s) research on the topic, the Cambridge academics sought to explore not only what the effects of experiencing a childhood bereavement were but also what factors might mitigate against that bereavement causing a child and his or her rails to diverge so significantly. Their list of 'mediating and moderating factors' includes cultural and personal aspects (such as the nature of the death itself as well as the rituals surrounding it), the family relationships, circumstances and many other dynamics at play before, during and after the event.

Focusing on cultural approaches to death briefly, it is worth noting that there is little in the research on place where death meets culture meets adolescence. According to University of Houston clinical professor Sandra Lopez, 'There is limited research to specifically address the influence of culture as it relates to adolescence and the experience of loss and grief.'[18]

She puts forward a number of suggestions for dealing with adolescent grief from a cultural perspective, not least of which is to start with understanding the impact of your own culture on your attitudes and beliefs surrounding death and grieving. She also highlights that adolescence can be seen not so much as a 'phase you're going through' but as a particular culture within a culture that needs to

---

17 C. McLaughlin, M. Lytje and C. Holliday, *Consequences of Childhood Bereavement in the Context of the British School System* (Cheltenham: Winston's Wish, 2019). Available at: https://wwwwinstonswish.org/wp-content/uploads/2019/06/COCB.pdf.

18 S. A. Lopez, Culture as an Influencing Factor in Adolescent Grief and Bereavement, *Prevention Researcher* 18(3) (2011): 10-13 at 13.

be treated as such, something she refers to as 'diversity within diversity'.

Lopez cites a 1995 publication by Rabbi Earl Grollman in which he outlines a list of suggestions for supporting grieving young people. Given the world we are living in his advice for dealing with those who have also experienced migration is worth a mention: 'With recent immigrants, validate other losses in their experience such as loss of their homeland, possessions, traditions, and family.'[19]

Like I say, it's complicated. However, rather than being deterred by the complexity at play in all of this, the caring teacher who is desperate to help but doesn't know where to start would probably do well to heed one other recommendation from Rabbi Grollman's list: to try 'Asking questions and listening rather than making conclusions.'

The desire to help that teachers have matched by not really knowing what to do is a key feature of the Winston's Wish research, so it is important to remember that schools doing something can and does make a difference, no matter how small. In the list of factors that can mitigate the effects of death and bereavement on young people, we find: 'Support from peers and other institutions and persons, such as grandparents and schools.'[20] Our experiences back this up too.

Despite the complexity of the circumstances surrounding the death – and other factors, including how a suicide has the potential to have a different sort of impact on the child compared to an unexpected death, the response to which may be different again from an anticipated death, and

19 Lopez, Culture as an Influencing Factor, p. 11. See also E. A. Grollman (ed.), *Bereaved Children and Teens: A Support Guide for Parents and Professionals* (Boston, MA: Beacon Press, 1995).

20 McLaughlin et al., *Consequences of Childhood Bereavement in the Context of the British School System*, p. 6.

how socio-economic status plays a part in how that child moves forward after the bereavement – please be assured that the actions of schools and the people in them do count.

This is what we found not only in the time immediately following our bereavement but also in the subsequent months – as described in *The Little Book of Bereavement for Schools* – and then years, as we are now setting out to describe briefly in this book. For this new iteration I have asked each of my children (young adults now, all of them, and making their own ways in the world and in various parts of the world too) to write a short piece updating the reader on how things have unfolded for them in their lives over the past decade or so.

After all, a bereavement is not an event. It is a process. You deal with the event. You then go through the process. It never ends. It evolves with you but it never ends. It is a process of accommodation, adapting your world to the parent-shaped hole in your life.

Which is where the concept of 9 + 1 comes in.

Talking to friend and Independent Thinking Associate Jim 'The Lazy Teacher' Smith a few weeks after my wife died, we were discussing his own experiences of living with childhood bereavement. I suggested sadly that life would never hold a 10 out of 10 moment again. From weddings to christenings, such magical family events would never be complete now, for any of us. His response has stayed with us and played out perfectly in my son's wonderful wedding in 2019. You will have '10' experiences; they will just be made up in a different way.

So, not 10 out of 10 but 9 + 1.

Our worlds are full of people who aren't there. But they are still the best of all possible worlds, if that is what we decide we want them to be. And it is no accident that one of the domains identified by the research into post-traumatic growth concerns what is called 'new possibilities'.[21]

From a very personal point of view, there is one other factor from the Winston's Wish research that has a relevance for schools, and that is 'The ability of the surviving parent to function and support the child after the death.'[22]

Hollywood loves a dead mum. From *Bambi* to *Chitty Chitty Bang Bang*, *Captain Fantastic* to *Billy Elliot*[23] *Cloudy with a Chance of Meatballs* to *Curly Sue*, to nearly everything based on a fairy tale – and, of course, *Love Actually* – it seems you can never trust mums to stick around for too long. Fathers, on the other hand, seem to be a great deal more dependable, but they do need all the help they can get.

Keeping on with the necessities of the old life, restoring broken childhoods, rebuilding new lives with new people in new places, being the keeper of the old memories (the good ones) and the creator of new ones (better ones) is hard work. And the girls' underwear section of M&S is the loneliest place in the world for a widowed father. As the surviving parent, you will do anything to make your children happy when you know you can't stop them being sad. So, whether you are at a school or a college, whether

21 McLaughlin et al., *Consequences of Childhood Bereavement in the Context of the British School System*, p. 39. See also: K. Taku, A. Cann, L. G. Calhoun and R. G. Tedeschi, The Factor Structure of the Posttraumatic Growth Inventory: A Comparison of Five Models Using Confirmatory Factor Analysis, *Journal of Traumatic Stress* 21(2) (2008): 158–164.

22 McLaughlin et al., *Consequences of Childhood Bereavement in the Context of the British School System*, p. 6.

23 Check out 'The Letter' from *Billy Elliot: The Musical* for an example of open-heart surgery.

you have been with the family and the siblings for years or you are dealing with a still-grieving child who has just shown up on your doorstep, remember that how you sup-port the remaining parent, as well as the still-grieving child, makes a massive difference.

And, as with all things, if you don't know what to do or how you can help, just ask. Knowing that you know you need to care and actually want to help, even if you don't know how, is so important. Having to ask for help is a task we all could have done without.

Talking of my own experience, one other striking aspect I have witnessed over the last few years is the manner in which bereavement changes more markedly the younger the bereaved child was at the point of the loss. With my youngest child, we went from pebbles[24] – you carry your grief in your pocket at all times and sometimes you take it out and hold it and are present with it and it's OK, and sometimes you put it away and get on with being a child – to puddles – whereas adults grieve in non-stop rivers, children grieve in intermittent puddles (and she still talks about 'puddly days' to describe days where the grief is still all too plainly felt).

After all, describing a death and the circumstances sur-rounding it in a way that makes sense to a nine-year-old is a very different process from describing it to a teenager or young adult, no matter how honest and frank you are. And, although none of us are fixed in time, and we all grow and evolve with our pain, the biggest changes take place over time for the youngest member of any family.

The best way I found to describe it is that it is like the child is sailing away from the coast, and the further they travel, the more of the land behind them they can see when they

---

24 The cover of *The Little Book of Bereavement for Schools* applies.

look back. And they see even more with each passing year, so each of those passing years brings more questions, more attempts to understand what can't really be understood, not rationally anyway, more pain, new pain, more accommodation to this terrible feeling of loss and difference and being alone.

And now they have to sit their GCSEs.

Of course, there are other bereavements than losing a parent, and the research that is growing in this area explores the effect of other losses including grandparents and siblings. Start with the paper commissioned by Winston's Wish, and by all means check out their website too and the various resources they offer. Other charities and agencies exist, of course, and all are keen to provide any support they can to you and the children in your care.

Since its publication in 2010, we know that *The Little Book of Bereavement for Schools* has proven to be very useful to schools and the people in them during some very difficult circumstances. Drawing on our experience and using it to help others has been a privilege for all four of us, and has given at least some purpose, if not reason, to what we have been through. We hope that this update will only serve to add to what that book has managed to achieve over the years and help it to keep on helping in the years to come.

In the original book, we asked Yvonne Holman to write us a foreword. She was then with a bereavement charity linked to a Suffolk hospice and had entered our lives within a few weeks of our loss. Her words still bear true:

> *The single most important message of the Little Book is the importance of giving your full attention to bereaved children in your school ... Each child will grieve in a unique way, but knowing about grief and bereavement will help you help them ... You will need courage, some knowledge and the*

backing of your colleagues to support a bereaved child in your class and school, but most of all you will need your humanity, tempered by professional skill.

Whatever you took from our first book, or whatever it is you will go on to take from this one, and wherever you start with the various organisations, research and resources we point you towards, the important thing is to start now, not to wait until the inevitable happens, again.

Or, as I wrote in 2010, 'Their world has just fallen apart. The least you can do is read this.'

III

WILLIAM

Unlike my sisters, I was almost at the end of my time in compulsory education when mum passed away. I was at sixth form college doing a BTEC (after walking out of another sixth form college offering A levels), and it would have been easy to have done badly. After all, I had plenty of excuses.

But it turned out that time at college was the most crucial of educational years, and I count myself as one of the lucky ones.

In my final year with mum, my first year of college, my grades weren't great, to be honest. True to type as a teen-age boy, I was plodding along, happy socialising with my new friends and happier still playing rugby, all of it miles away from the challenges I faced at home, mentally if not geographically.

At that time I was lucky enough to have a great relationship with my head of year who, when mum passed away, sat with me and my dad and laid it out in front of me with that combination of care and brutal frankness that great teachers have. After all, my choices were quite straightforward. I could carry on as I was and end up with mediocre grades way below my potential. Or I could start again once my head was in the right space and work towards the grades I was capable of achieving without the current distractions (not sure how). Or, somehow, I could find a way to leave 'home at home' and buckle down to my studies when I was at college.

To be fair, I had tried to do this both at secondary school and at college, but it was always easier said than done. I'm certain that if you had asked any of my previous teachers from Year 4 onwards whether they knew what hell (to be brutally frank) I'd be going home to on a daily basis, they would have been clueless. The thing is, to this day, I'm still not sure if them not knowing about my home life was a good thing or a bad thing.

But I'll come to that later.

I chose the last of the three options my head of year had spelled out to me, and I managed to get myself up from three merits to three distinctions in my final year, which opened the door to a top-flight university for me. If it hadn't been for this honesty from my head of year, I doubt I'd have ended up at any university, let alone a really good one.

Of course, the abrupt change in my home life as a result of mum's death also contributed to me being able to focus on myself and my studies much more, now that I needed less time to help with mum and my sisters. But how can you say to people that your mum dying was a great help with your grades?

I think something else that was helpful in my education back then was that I am not only outgoing and open, but I will also speak up if I think something needs sorting (hence me walking out of the first college I went to: boring A levels taught in a boring way – who needs that in their life?). Perhaps, though, there are lots of students who are facing similar difficulties but who are too quiet to say anything and might end up getting lost in the system. How are schools and colleges making sure that everyone is listened to, even when they don't speak out?

I've never heard from my head of year, or indeed the college, since that time. I'm not really sure what I'd want them to say or ask at this stage, but a phone call to see how I'd got on would have made me feel good, and I would have let them know that they did help, especially with everything I'd been through. I'd have happily spoken about it and, who knows, if they'd needed me to talk to any student who was also going through what I'd experienced, I probably would have obliged.

University was a totally different ball game though. I'd gone to a university where I knew no one, breaking the mould and not following any of my mates from college – partly because they didn't get the grades needed and partly to escape people who knew too much. One set of such memories in a new place is enough.

Preparing for university was an exciting time. My dad was encouraging me to take a year out, sit on a beach, drink beer and have some time for me. But after so much chaos and hurt what I needed was a bit of structure and a new challenge. I remember receiving my first letter from the university, asking all about me so they could ensure I was paired with someone compatible in a shared room – hobbies, dislikes, the usual. Even if there had been an option to write that I was 'one parent down' (there wasn't), I doubt I'd have written that. But, of course, simple things like watching my friends have both parents visit frequently hurt. It was a constant reminder of what I didn't have. This is something I know that my youngest sister struggles with at university now. Maybe cross-referencing 'roomies' and 'corridors' with 'frequency of parental visits' and 'number of parents involved' would help.

I had chosen to go to university in the UK while the rest of my family had gone to live abroad as they worked to rebuild a new life, which meant not being sure where to go during term breaks and over the summer, which wasn't easy. But no one really asks where you're going anyway. The summer work I had back then came with accommodation so, of course, I wasn't on the streets. But maybe it wouldn't do a caring institution any harm to check where their students are going to live when they're not at university.

Three years went by so quickly, as I'm sure it does for everyone in higher education. No one there was much the wiser about what I'd been through, but that is what I wanted at the time. While it might not be right for everyone – and I'm aware that mental illness and suicide are big issues at UK universities currently – I was happy enough to fly under the radar. That said, if anyone had ever asked me to speak about what I'd experienced, to help others in a similar position, I would have said yes. But no one did.

It's only as I look back now, twelve years since my mum died, ten years since I graduated and twenty years from my earliest memories of living with a poorly mum, that I realise things could have been very different. Different in that it would have helped a great deal if issues around mental health and then bereavement could have had the acceptance they now seem to have acquired, even though that is only in the past five years or so. Being able to talk openly outside of our family home would have been beneficial. And different too because who knows what would have happened to me if I had not had the family support that I needed during my childhood – unconditional support that helped me to have the strength to carry on when I needed it the most.

I do worry about all those kids who didn't have that support, the ones who were lost in the crowd. Where are they now? Are they pursuing the same path as their parent? They will probably have, or will soon be having, kids themselves. Are they lifting them up or pulling them down? As an adult now myself, I know that it is adults who have the power to help break such cycles. And they do so by supporting the children in their care. Reading this book is a good start. Thank you.

IV
OLIVIA

Looking back, I don't remember there being any particular action or gesture that displayed to me that the school wanted to support me or my family after mum passed away. Maybe there was stuff going on behind the scenes that I didn't know about. What I did see was a lot of sympathetic glances across the corridors from both teachers and classmates, but, apart from my immediate friends, there didn't seem to be anybody taking responsibility for supporting me.

In other words, when I went back to school it seemed like nothing had happened.

But it had.

Feeling ignored and not overtly supported by the place in which you spend the most amount of time as a child was difficult. However, on the positive side, it was also refreshing. Home was a dark place at that time and school almost became a break from death, a place where I could feel 'normal', at least for the day.

One of the initial stages of bereavement immediately after losing someone you love is denial. This is what is to be expected, I suppose, but it is not a healthy place to remain. Thankfully I had a family that was prone to talking about feelings, so I had the best of both worlds. I could experience a semblance of normality at school, like nothing had happened, and just try to be an average teenage girl (as if being a teenage girl in an English secondary school isn't hard enough). And then, at the end of the day, I would return home to family life and be able to express the hurt and anger I was then experiencing.

It had been the same before mum died with everything that was going on. For me, a policy of 'Home is home and school is school' helped me to navigate both worlds as best I could. While this worked for me, if anything can be said to work at such a time, I know that not all families communicate as openly as mine did. For those kids who get ignored and are not given the opportunity to express their loss, either at home or at school, such a situation can only be detrimental to their grieving process.

I soon passed through the stage of denial – although nothing seems to pass very quickly at a time like this – and became increasingly more emotional and desperate to speak out about what I was going through. Except it didn't seem as if anyone at school was interested in hearing what I had to say. Again, maybe because I had seemed 'OK' a few weeks before (I suppose looking OK is one of the side effects of denial), everyone thought I was simply getting on with my life, and so there was, as the phrase goes, 'nothing to see here'.

But there was.

As we started our new lives and travels in the years following that terrible time, I went to a number of schools and colleges in various parts of the world. Unfortunately, the scant support I had received at the school I was attending when the incident happened diminished to what seemed to be no support in later schools. Naturally, I didn't walk in like Paddington with a label attached to my coat with the words 'Please look after this demi-orphan'[1] on it. But it would have been really helpful if there had been a department or even a person who could have given me the opportunity to disclose what had happened, who had been trained properly (and had read this book) and whose role it was to be there for children who had gone through a loss like mine.

---

1   Demi-orphan is the term we use in our family. Judging by the way others look at us when we say it, I don't think it's an actual thing. But, hey, you do what you need to do to get by …

Throughout my time at the various schools I attended, it was not uncommon for teachers to simply ask me, 'What happened?' Although I understand they meant well, questions such as these can be quite devastating, as it only takes a few words for you to essentially re-live the experience again. What's more, as a young child it is difficult to comprehend what actually did happen. And what happens next when the child replies, 'Well, my mum was really unwell and then she drowned in the bath'? Where does a teacher with no training and no real clue go then? Where would *you* go?

Remember, it doesn't matter what happened, only that it did happen.

V

PHOEBE

'I'm really sorry but mummy died. Mummy isn't coming home.'

Those were the words that engulfed the little nine-year-old I once was, while looking down at my father who was kneeling in front of me in my head teacher's office. Maybe the reason why this school went on to become such an essential place as I came to terms with my loss was because I was in the safety of my head teacher's office when I found out the worst news of my life. Or maybe it's because of the support and care we received from the staff there even before my mum passed away, not to mention afterwards.

In the many stressful months prior to, at the time of and after my mum's death, my primary school was the most caring and the most humanely understanding of schools – a school that just 'got it'. They got that all families are different. They got that all families have challenges. They got that there are children in some families who are not fortunate enough to live a normal 'get home from school, do all my homework, eat smiley-face potatoes, watch *Barney & Friends* and go to bed' life.

So, they got that life for me was not quite normal. It was about trying to hold on to being an 'annoying nine-year-old'[1] while also trying to hang on to a mum who was not at all well.

Within days of mum's passing, my school encouraged my classmates to create sympathy cards. I remember one specifically saying, 'Sorry your mum's dead', and that was it. But it was something, and something always meant more than nothing. With this kind gesture, and the most beautiful bouquet of flowers sent on behalf of the staff, our home felt somewhat less lonely in the loneliest time of our

1   The measure dad used to judge if I was OK. The more annoying (i.e. normal) I was, the happier he was.

lives. They had not only supported me, and offered support to my dad and my family, but they had also helped a class of young children to understand how to react in a time of death, how to offer condolences and how to be aware of others' suffering and pain. This was so important.

Although I could talk at length about how well my primary school handled the situation, both before and after my mum's death, it is also important to shed light on the times when school caused the pain in my heart to feel just that bit more acute.

I didn't even know that was possible, but it was.

After a school that had handled things so well, it would become apparent over time that some of the schools I would attend subsequently would fail to support me and my loss and the heartache of missing my mother. What hardly anyone seemed to understand was that my grief would grow and change as I grew and changed. For example, I might be sadder or angrier on Mother's Day this year than I was last year.[2]

And, no, I will *never* be 'over it'.

One of my most painful memories after I lost my mum was being made to sit in on a Mother's Day assembly, still aged nine but at a new primary school I was by then attending, followed by a session making Mother's Day cards. I had felt alone before but this feeling of utter loneliness was new to me. I had no mummy to make a card for, and my school had left me to drown as this knowledge became ever more painfully apparent. This was when I realised that not every school, and not every teacher, was going to have the same shaped heart as the one I had known at the beginning of this particular journey.

---

2   When you have spent time abroad you learn that there are actually two Mother's Days a year, which seems very cruel indeed.

But that is really no excuse.

Although others' lives continue, my family and I are still faced with the missing piece of the jigsaw – her empty seat at the table on special occasions, the guilt of continuing traditions without her, the ache of her absence continuing to grow in our lives. But having at least one individual (albeit a teacher) remember an anniversary and ask how I am has always made a 'special' day (*the* anniversary, a birthday, Mother's Day, etc.) more bearable and somewhat less lonely.

To be honest, I have felt let down by many of my teachers, as they often fail to understand that there are so many emotions and feelings that I can't explain but just have to ride with. If I get angry over burnt toast, then know that I'm not sensitive, I'm just grieving, and it sucks. If I do badly in a test, I'm not stupid, I'm still just grieving, and it sucks.

Some days I may choose to be happy because, well, who doesn't want to be happy? But it still sucks.

Over the past twelve years of being a grieving child (I don't think there is a past tense for grieving because it is not something that is ever in the past) the biggest struggle has been the loneliness it brings. This is even more intense at university, which comes with a sense of having to get on with it. It comes with a sense of having to be an 'adult' and to put my childhood grief aside, but 'puddly' days still happen.[3] Twelve years on doesn't mean I've had twelve years to get over it. It means I've had twelve years to feel it more, especially when it comes to, for example, living with university friends who get to go out with their mums on Mother's Day.

But there are some wonderful people working in education. I have fantastic university tutors who 'get it' too. I

---

3   See page 21.

made it clear to my course leader at the beginning of my time here that my loss still affects me, and the subsequent love and understanding I have received has been amazing. I know that I have made her proud simply by attending university and succeeding, not just surviving.

#proudness as we say.

So, please know that this book is for every phase of the education system, whether you are a primary school teacher, a high school teacher or even a university lecturer. Remember that for young men and women, such as myself, our loss is part of us. It is part of who we were, who we are and who we are becoming. And as I'm currently trying to get my degree, there is a lot more to it than being at university during term time and returning to 'normality' in-between times. I'm trying to make my way, and, most of all, I'm still trying to make sense of what has happened, in the same way that all those others in my position will be trying to make sense of their world too. After all, there is no one specific framework for loss. Each individual is different and you, as a professional, must be prepared to adapt to whoever is in front of you.

Where do you start? (Reading this book is already a good start, so thank you for that.) You can't fill the hole in the hearts of people like me or take away our pain, but there are things you can do to make it slightly more bearable for us on days when everything seems too much.

Respond at all times with love and support. Notice when we are there. Notice when we are not there. Offer to sit with us. Maybe listen to a song that is just too hard for us to hear alone. Offer us a cuppa. Take the time to learn about our pain, even if it just means listening. Take time to ask about our lost loved one. And, most importantly, allow us to find a reason for our pain and choose happiness again.

VI
THE LESSONS

The following lessons first appeared in *The Little Book of Bereavement for Schools,* which was published in 2010. Rereading them brings back many memories. They are still as valid as ever.

ONE

As soon as the death is known to the school, have a senior member of staff talk to the immediate classmates about what has happened. Stamp out any gossip and offer support for those who may be affected.

Ignorance is a vacuum that gossip quickly fills. And gossip – lies perpetrated by people too lazy to wait for the truth and too shallow to want it anyway – is a very destructive force in anyone's life, let alone a child's, at this time.

What is more, gossip, tittle-tattle and fanciful invention quickly take root as received truths in the classroom, the playground, the staffroom and then in kitchens at home and from there on into the virtual social world that most children inhabit. So, while the child is away dealing with the end of their world as they know it, a whole tangle of lies is being created behind their back.

As if they don't have enough to deal with.

In my elder daughter's secondary school, one member of the senior leadership team was a personal friend. When I went to break the news to my daughter, and then take her home, I made sure that the office informed him of what had happened. I found out later that he had immediately called together my daughter's tutor group, informed them of the facts of the situation and, with a seriousness and firmness that made a significant impression on the class, instructed them that he would not tolerate any gossip or rumour-mongering from them and that they would have him to deal with if he discovered any.

What he was also able to do at that moment by using his authority and his honesty was to offer support to the students in my daughter's class who were genuinely upset by my wife's death, many of whom knew her personally.

To know that all this was being dealt with by him in such a professional, firm and caring manner was of huge benefit to my daughter as well as to me. It also gave a framework, a structure, that helped the other students know what to do and how to react in a situation in which most adults don't know what to do or how to react.

I remember when I was ten, the father of one of my best friends died suddenly and again, before the gossip kicked in, our form tutor gathered us together and, fighting back her own tears, explained what had happened and what we were to do. I remember it clearly, even though it was almost forty-five years ago.

Teaching is one of the most powerful jobs on the planet at the best of times. In dire times like this, done well, it has the potential to be one of the most dignified and supportive.

TWO

Send a condolence card and encourage classmates to do the same. Saying 'I didn't know what to do' and doing nothing is a form of moral cowardice – and why should you be let off the hook? No one else knows what to do either.

We received cards and emails from people every day and they stopped on the morning of my wife's funeral. At a time when what you are going through is incredibly personal and closed off from the world, such gestures are tremendously supportive and played a huge part in helping us through those first few numb, painful (and I know that is an oxymoron but that's how it is) days and weeks.

Within a day of my friend's actions at the secondary school we were receiving cards and flowers from my daughter's friends and the occasional, appropriate, visit.

My younger daughter was at a small rural infant school and while I do not know exactly how the children were told about what had happened, within a day or so we received a bundle through the letterbox. Inside were cards designed and painted by every single child in the school addressed to my daughter and although the messages were rather abrupt at times – 'Sorry your mum's dead. Gavin' – the heart was always in the right place. In terms of doing the right thing, they were *exactly* the right thing. In this way, not only did the children in the whole school have a structured way of responding to the situation, but they also created something that made a difference to their classmate's life.

The infant school also sent a card from the head teacher on behalf of the staff, which was a lovely gesture – whereas the secondary school didn't because 'We didn't know what to do'. One or two of my friends acted in a similar way and I couldn't help but feel disappointed and let down by them. Nobody knows what to do. There is nothing you can do. Nothing anyone can do. But doing nothing is never the right thing to do. A card, an email, a baked cake, a text, anything – no matter how futile you feel it may be – is better than nothing.

Ninety-nine per cent of the cards contained the words, 'Let me know if there's anything I can do.' It's a cliché but it's a start. One of the cards contained words to the effect, 'Rather than saying is there anything we can do, we want to be specific about what we *will* do.' They then went on to offer us a weekend away at a time to suit us doing rock climbing and an assault course in the Cheshire countryside. We went several months later and it was *absolutely* the right thing to do. Doing the 'Leap of Faith' from the top of a pole thirty feet up onto a trapeze in the crisp November sunshine was something that my girls will never forget.

On the subject of what to do or not to do, a quick word about the funeral. Go! Unless there are specific instructions not to, ensure that at least one suitable someone is there to represent the whole school, such as a member of the management team or the tutor or the head of year or all three of them. Furthermore, encourage the classmates most affected by the loss to attend the funeral too if they are old enough, possibly going with a parent if necessary. Although the grieving family will probably not register who was actually there during the ceremony (it was the first time I had seen those special cards that the undertaker distributes which each person fills in and leaves behind as a record of who was there), the feeling of support and love from a group of people who are all there for you and for the person you are all remembering is very powerful. My children's friends being there for them was as much a support for my children as my friends being there for me.

On top of that, remember that funerals serve a very powerful purpose in helping everyone to come to terms with the loss and get off the starting blocks as it were when it comes to grieving. Denial is so much harder when you have seen the coffin.

THREE

When the child comes back to school talk to them (but don't patronise them). Ask them how they would like their teachers to act.

Sometimes coming back to school is the best thing the child can do – the first rung on the ladder to getting their life back again (although the ladder goes on forever). For some children, though, going back to school will feel like too much too soon. The problem is that maybe they won't know that until they get there.

When the child comes back you have to do everything you can to make sure that this will not be a normal day for anyone, not least the child, and then do everything you can to make sure it is a normal day.

Speak to the staff and let them know what is happening. In my experience, many will not know what to say and will either overlook the death (in my son's college, while the tutor was brilliant, the rest of his teachers simply ignored the situation) or just give sad, sympathetic looks that, although probably well-meant, don't help. The child doesn't need pity from adults; they need strength, consistency and understanding. And 'How are you?' is not a good question either. The child will probably reply with 'I'm fine' because they know that is what people want to hear, but, in reality, they want to scream how it really is. A simple but sincere, 'I was really sorry to hear about the death of your mother' is fine. Another strategy is to deflect your sympathy towards another family member. 'How is your sister getting along?' or 'How is your father coping?' can be a useful way to show you care.

Sometimes people leap in with a story of their own loss. This is not helpful at this stage, or at least not if you divert the focus onto yourself entirely. Our experience was that we didn't want to hear anything about anyone else during this early stage of grief. It was an unnecessary annoyance and a selfish act by the perpetrator. 'I know how you are feeling because I went through it too at your age' can be useful and, at some point in the future, the child may want to come back to you on it so you can explore things further. But for now, use your experience to know what to do and what not to do. That is all you can do at this point.

Of course, the above is just our opinion based on our experience and you might find a child in your care thinks differently. You can always ask them. They may have an idea and that may well be 'Treat me normally', or they may have no idea at all, in which case make sure you have a plan anyway. Part of this should also be ensuring that, at any time of the day, the child knows that they can just get up and go to a safe place without asking or explaining. This may be your office or an unused meeting room. Make sure that all staff know about this, and if the child leaves part way through their lesson to let this happen without fuss or hindrance.

Grief is like standing on a beach and being hit by waves. You don't know when they are going to hit you but you know they will, and when they do there is nothing you can do to stop it. Make sure the child knows they can go to the safe place whenever they feel they want to and no one will make a big thing of it. In fact, everyone will be really understanding. It might be that you nominate a friend to escort them there but then leave them on their own if that is what they want. Nominating that person in advance avoids the crush of girls if you ask, on the spot, for a volunteer or the awkward silence from the boys as they stare at their pencils.

Make sure all adults – teaching and non-teaching – are keeping an eye out for the child too and ensure that you are reassuring the parent that this is what is happening. To know that so many people are keeping a discreet and caring watch over your child at such a time is very reassuring for the parent and allows them to get on with their own life, such as it is, at the same time.

FOUR

Teach other children to know what to say and how to handle things.

In my experience, most adults haven't got a clue how to act and what to say when someone has died, but then why should they? No one has taught them and, culturally, we treat death like Belgium. We know it's not far away but no one wants to talk about it, let alone go there. If, as adults, we've gone through our entire lives avoiding facing up to it, then how does it feel for the children in your class-rooms who suddenly have to deal with it?

The more you can talk about dying with the children, before a real-life death takes place in your school, the bet-ter, in my view. There are many opportunities for doing this, using vehicles such as RE, circle time, Philosophy for Children, personal, social, health and economic education and even history or English to share stories, explore beliefs and convictions, and identify a common vocabulary for talking about death. From the death of someone famous to the death of a grandparent or the death of a pet, all of these are opportunities to start opening up about the topic in your school and to start breaking down some of the taboos. This will make life just that little bit easier when (as opposed to 'if') something terrible happens at your school.

And when I say vocabulary I mean it literally. Like John Cleese in the Dead Parrot Sketch, often people can't even articulate the word 'dead' and so resort to that great British habit of the euphemism. Telling a class that so and so's father has 'gone to sleep now' is not helpful to anyone except you (although better than 'pushing up the daisies' or 'fallen off his perch'). That said, 'has died' is less brutal than 'is dead'.

Give the children some examples of what they could say such as, 'I'm really sorry to hear about the death of your ...' or 'I'm really sorry. You know I'll always be there for you.' Make sure they don't put any undue pressures on the grieving child to be either happy or sad. My children were asked repeatedly in the years immediately following their mother's death why they weren't crying, the implication arrived at by simple childish logic being that their mother can't be dead then. As if they were making the whole thing up. The first time this happened my youngest came home very distressed. They began to deal with it better after we had talked it through, but in the years that followed they still came home with the occasional, resigned, 'It happened again ...'

Let the children know that at times the child will want to be alone, at times they will want their friends around them, at times they will seem happy, even laughing, at times they will suddenly burst into tears or go off in a rage. Let them know that such changes can happen very quickly and that they are perfectly natural. Don't let them think that if the grieving child is laughing then they have forgotten. Or that if they are crying then they should be given a hanky to make them stop. Crying is good, natural and useful. And can't be stopped anyway. The classmates need to learn what it is to be an unconditional friend at this stage, being there for the grieving child no matter how they act and react.

FIVE

School can be the place to escape from what is going on at home ('Home is home and school is school'). Respect that wish as much as possible.

As anyone who has taught children from troubled backgrounds (which is all educators) should know, sometimes schools can be the only safe, reliable, consistent place in their world. Yet the new convergence of social care, parental involvement, health support and education means that school's place as a haven of normality and an escape from the troubles and tribulations of life at home is under threat.

During the period before my wife's death there was a great deal of stress and distress at home. Any family dealing with serious illness, especially a terminal one (and, yes, I include mental illness in that list), will experience this. For many teachers, they have no idea what sort of scenario that child comes from and returns to each day. The fact that they turn up on time, washed, in uniform, with their homework even partly done is a testament to that child's resilience and determination to be, well, normal.

While some children may need support at school to deal with all that the world is throwing at them at that time, others may not want it. It could be that such an intrusion may be detrimental to their well-being. My younger daughter benefited hugely from the opportunities she had to sit down and talk one-to-one with the visiting school nurse, and we are all extremely grateful for the professional, unconditional, non-judgemental support she gave my daughter. Time with this nurse was the safe place my daughter needed both before and after her mother's death, the nurse herself providing something concrete and anchored in a world that was becoming neither.

My elder daughter, however, was very different. She used school as a way to 'forget' all that was going on at home. The phrase 'Home is home and school is school' is one of hers and it was her way of surviving the ordeal of the illness and her mother's death. School was where she could be normal and she needed that very much. Whether the difference is an age thing or just a reflection of the difference in their personalities I cannot say. But there is a difference and you cannot have a one-size-fits-all policy in such matters.

How will you know which one to apply and when? Firstly, ask the child. Secondly, liaise with the parent. I certainly knew which was the preferred strategy of each of my three children. Thirdly, use your professional acuity. Keep your eyes and ears open. And, fourthly, keep asking (without nagging) so the child knows that there will be help as soon as it is needed at school. They only need to ask.

SIX

Grieving is mentally and physically exhausting.

Have you ever watched a weepie movie and come out of the cinema all limp and exhausted? Being emotional takes up a great deal of physical and mental energy. Now imagine crying like that day after day for weeks. And the times you are not crying are because you are in too much pain to cry – and you wish you would cry because it makes you feel a little better, but not much – or because you are asleep. Although then you often wake yourself up crying. Or wake up after a lovely dream where everything was as good as it used to be and then, as the reality of your new bereavement hits you, you just want to go back to sleep but you can't. So you cry.

Grieving is an incredibly tiring process, as exhausting as it is relentless in the early days and weeks. Your body clock is out. Your daily routines are out. Your appetite is out. Your sleeping patterns are out. Your whole cycle of sleeping, waking, working, resting and everything else associated with daily life has been turned upside down and inside out and you feel you will never be normal again.

What's more, the process of grieving can – should – involve a great deal of talking. It certainly did in our house. And talking about what has happened and how everyone is feeling will find its own time and place and is no respecter of bedtimes. Especially when, for the child, going to bed is the worst time of day, the time when they feel most alone.

What this means is that the child may not be particularly alert in class, may not have done their homework, may not even be able to stay awake in a particular lesson, may not be able to concentrate, may be irascible or erratic, or any manner of indicators of someone who is overwhelmingly fatigued.

Having somewhere, then, that the child can go if they just need to grab a quick nap when they suddenly feel the need is very useful (and as sleep is such welcome respite from being awake at a time like this it is a shame to waste it). Reinforcing with other staff members that the physical demands of grieving mean that the child may not have finished their homework or be up to that game of sport or want to go out and play is useful too. Ensure that the child is eating as well as possible. They may not be eating at home or even be having the opportunity to eat with all that is going on. They may not even want to eat at lunch-time so having a sandwich put by for them and letting them eat it part way through the afternoon may be beneficial.

The key here, as with so much of helping children who are grieving, is staying alert and being flexible. Keep an eye on what their needs are and then respond to those needs as creatively and quickly as possible without making a fuss.

Your professionalism, though, also demands that you find a balance here, as you will see in Lesson Seven.

SEVEN

Be tolerant of homework and other work commitments – evenings may well be spent grieving and talking, not working. Agree work commitments with the child, though, and be firm but caring as you try to ensure they don't get too far behind (and thereby add a feeling of failure to their grieving).

Your homework on the rain cycle, for example, will not be top of a bereaved child's list for a while so you must be tolerant. For those children who are using school to escape the distress of what is happening at home, it is when they leave the school gates that the work really starts.

As I mentioned before, evenings and nights will be spent grieving in whatever shape that takes. If the child is fortunate, it will take the form of plenty of love and cuddles and talking. Speaking honestly, openly and without being judged is so important at this stage. The taboo nature of death, not to mention the other baggage that many families carry with them, means they never actually communicate and can remain trapped in a terrifying Pinteresque world. It means that often the death is not talked about and the remaining parent may well become 'stuck', unable to let go, unable to move on, unable to be of any real support to their children. This leaves the child lost and alone as they try to deal with their own feelings, which means that there is even less chance of them being able to concentrate on their school work.

Falling behind at school or college will make a bad situation worse, especially if the child is in Key Stage 4 or 5. What are you going to do to ensure that the child has the space and time to grieve without undue pressure to make their brain do things it can't yet do, like concentrate or remember things or care about that homework on the rain cycle, but at the same time exert just enough pressure to make sure that the child stays, if not on track, then not too far from it?

My son was similar to my elder daughter in his approach when it came to keeping home and college separate as much as possible, although the nature of a further education college is more hands-off on the whole anyway. However, he had a tutor who would speak to him often, who spoke to me as was necessary and who we both knew was there if we needed her. In this relaxed but caring way she steered my son through his time at the college, putting just enough pressure on him to achieve the grades he was capable of, without letting him off the hook and using his home life as an excuse for not handing in work. She also knew when to ease back and just be there for him as a sad and lost young person, not just as a student.

One morning my son and I went into college together and sat down with her as she went through every one of his assignments and outlined where he was, how far behind he was, what he needed to do to catch up and what scores he needed to achieve his target grades for each area. The three of us left that meeting with a copy of this sheet, a plan and a sense of reassurance that it was achievable. My son knew exactly where he stood and what he had to do. He also knew that, although he was the one who had to put in the work, he was not alone.

EIGHT

Talk to the spouse if they come to the school. Show them you know and care and are there to help. Don't just ignore them because you don't know what to say. That is more moral cowardice.

The bottom may have fallen out of the child's world following the death of a mother or father, but it is not a bed of roses for the surviving partner either. If that parent then makes the effort to come to school, to show his or her face – when all they really want to do is curl up and join their spouse, as the awful realisation dawns that the responsibility for their children now lies entirely in their hands, no longer shared – then the least you can do is be supportive.

My elder daughter went back to school the week following her mother's death, partly as a result of her 'Home is home and school is school' strategy and partly because it was Activities Week so there were no 'normal' lessons as such. During that week she became involved in a big musical production with a presentation to parents on the Thursday. If she had the strength to do this then the least I could do was go along and support her. She had lost one parent; I don't want her ever to feel as though she has lost both.

As the crowd of parents and children edged their way through the double doors of the school sports hall where the performance was being held, my daughter's head of year was standing at the entrance welcoming in parents. As I passed, even though I was inches from her, she could not bring herself to look at me, much less speak to me. Once inside, sitting there among a crowd of strangers, I felt like the most alone person in the world, like the empty eye of a hurricane, cut off, lost. On the way out I saw the head teacher who became too emotional too talk and just looked at me with tears in her eyes. At least she looked me in the eye. I was overwhelmed with a need to get out of there and so rudely pushed my way through the crowd and back into the summer evening air. I just wanted to collect my daughter and go back home to our sad, safe space.

So, what can we learn from that evening? When you are grieving, getting out of bed is an ordeal, let alone attending a school play, so be mindful of the enormous effort the parent is making and the strain they are under. The head of year later told my teacher friend that she felt really bad but didn't know what to say. *She* felt bad! As I say at the start of this lesson, doing nothing is moral cowardice. However hard it is for you, it is so much harder for them, so just get on with it and 'do your day job' as they say. And being emotional yourself is OK. It shows empathy and connection.

And if you see them sitting in the school hall looking lost and alone, just go up to them, touch them on the back and say a simple, 'You must be so proud of your daughter, Mr …' or 'She's done so well hasn't she? And don't worry, we'll keep an eye on her' or something equally caring, acknowledging and reassuring.

As a footnote to this lesson, what support are you able to engineer for the grieving parent from other parents who may have gone through the same loss? In the school car park, as I was hurrying myself and my daughter home after the performance, I met a woman who had a girl in the same year as my daughter who had lost her husband in tragic circumstances several years earlier. She was the first person to call on me after the news broke of my wife's death and she remained in contact in just the right way afterwards. In the car park she introduced me to her 'new' husband (they had already been married for several years by then, but 'new' sounds so much better than 'current'). She knew what it was like and, importantly, she was able to reassure me that life goes on, that happiness returns, that things will get better, that I would find love again. She was right.

NINE

Keep on talking to the child and letting them know you still remember, even just in small ways.

Talking is like Germolene. It takes the pain away a little bit and helps just a little bit and gives you something to do while the real healing process is taking place. And it is so much better than doing nothing. Make sure the child has every opportunity to talk about what has happened and their feelings about it, not just immediately after their parent's death but in the weeks, months and, if possible, years after the tragedy.

There are two magic ingredients here too – having somewhere to talk and having someone to talk to.

As I mentioned before, my younger daughter had her school nurse, and she continued seeing her a couple of times a week for as long as she could, including when she moved to middle school a few months after her mother's death where the nurse picked up the reins again.

My elder daughter went to the school nurse once and that was all she needed. Although she could have seen her at school the policy of keeping home and school separate meant that she did not want this. Instead we arranged the visit at the local doctors' surgery, where they spent an hour or so talking. Although my daughter was happy to go she didn't feel she wanted to do it again, and that was fine by me. At least she knew the school nurse's face and where the door was, and that the door would always be open and the face would always be kind.

During this visit the nurse described to my daughter a useful way to understand the difference between the way small children grieve and the way older children and adults mourn. Adults, she explained, grieve in rivers where they are fully immersed in their grief for an extended period of time following a death. Little children, on the other hand, grieve in puddles. In other words, the child moves in and out of their grief like someone stepping in puddles. Sometimes they are fine. Sometimes terribly, albeit briefly, sad. It was a really helpful analogy, and even now my younger daughter will talk about having 'puddle moments' or a 'puddly day' when things have all got too much for her again. We help her through it by listening supportively and then we all know it will pass, until the next time.

Sometimes the chat you need is not an in-depth, soul-wrenching, open all the floodgates, better out than in heart-to-heart. You just want someone to say, 'How is it going now?' or 'How is your father/brother/sister getting on?' or 'What are you planning for your holidays this year?' Something that starts a conversation about day-to-day life without the deceased parent and shows that you haven't forgotten and that you care. Even, if well timed, 'What do you miss most about your mother?' can be useful and, you may be surprised to learn, doesn't always lead to tears.

Sometimes people worry about mentioning the deceased person's name in case the bereaved relative has forgotten and they don't want to open up the wound again and make them cry. If the only thing you learn from this book is the following then it will be worthwhile:

The bereaved person *never* forgets about the person they are missing, and the fact that you mention them by name means that person is still, in some way, alive. Because of this it is *always* the best thing you can do. And if it makes that person cry, it doesn't matter. Crying is not wrong. In fact, it is amazing how much of daily life can be conducted with tears streaming down your face.

TEN

Remember the anniversaries.

When you are grieving time is a double-edged sword. On the one hand it seems to stop and you are desperate for it to get going again so you can make a start on rebuilding your life. On the other hand, like dropping someone off at a bus stop, the further on you travel, the further from them you end up. Suddenly you cannot recall their face or the sound of their voice or their smell, and you begin to realise that your story is now being written such that the person who had been everything to you is now just a name and an emotion. No more.

But once every 365 days things change.

The anniversary of the death, especially the first one, is a very difficult time. Especially if it is linked to other anniversaries, as in my household: the last time my three children saw their mother or the last time I saw my wife, which was several days before her actual death.

For the first anniversary I took all three of them out of school and college for the day. Although none of the establishments had a problem with this, I did still have to fill in a 'holiday form' from the secondary school and, supposedly, obtain the head teacher's permission to do this. Surely there must be a form that can be filled in for absence that does not say 'holiday' on the front and make you feel like you are doing your child's education a terrible disservice by taking them out for the day? Anyway, we went to London to see the matinee performance of *Les Misérables* as part of our 'better out than in' policy. I wanted to address the grief head on and spend the day together but not moping. (As a surprise I then bought them tickets for *Billy Elliot*, thinking something a bit more light-hearted at the end of the day would help. I forgot that Billy had lost his mother. And then there was the 'Dear Billy' song … Talk about exhausting. But anyway, like we say, better out than in.)

Make a note in your diary of the anniversary of the death and, on the day, make contact with the child somehow to let them know you know. If you let other staff know too that will help both in terms of watching out for the child during the day and also letting them know that none of you have forgotten.

And to show you really care, don't just remember the first anniversary. Although they become less painful with the passing of time (so we're told), the anniversaries over the coming years are still days of heightened emotions and intense memories. Even now, however many anniversaries later, there are still tears, a sense of dread as June comes back round and a sigh of relief as it passes again, for another year.

Something to bear in mind here is the question of transition. While my son and my elder daughter were at the same educational establishment on the first anniversary of their mother's death, my youngest had changed schools. She had gone from her infant school to a middle school but from there to a primary school because we had moved house. Despite explaining the situation to the primary school head teacher and the class teacher they just didn't get it and never engaged with my daughter and her grieving. Maybe it was because they had not lived through the drama and the trauma of my wife's death and its impact on a school, or maybe it was because they just didn't really care about their children in the way that I know other schools would have done. Who knows? Either way, the first is an excuse and the second is unforgivable. I remember speaking to my Independent

Thinking associate and friend Julie Rees who is a primary head teacher and the author of *The Little Book of Values*.[1] She would have been 'all over' my daughter and her grieving in a highly caring and supportive way, and was appalled at the lack of interest shown by my daughter's primary school (and don't get me started on Mother's Day! That's for the next lesson ...).

To what extent are you aware of the particular situations of the children joining your school and what anniversaries are there to watch out for? And if the child is leaving your school, what can you do to ensure the new school 'gets the message'? These are vital questions for you during transition or handover between schools, and ones you need to get right.

---

1   J. Rees, *The Little Book of Values: Educating Children to Become Thinking, Responsible and Caring Citizens* (Carmarthen: Crown House Publishing, 2009).

ELEVEN

Be aware of areas you may cover in the curriculum that may bring back memories (Mother's Day, Father's Day, birthdays, life after death in RE, areas that touch on any illness such as cancer or mental illness and so on).

'We won't be doing anything special on Mother's Day,' said my daughter's primary school teacher. I was surprised by this response to my question about the day. I just wanted her to be aware of what had happened: that it would be my daughter's first Mother's Day without a mother and to tread thoughtfully. It seemed reasonable to me and although I was surprised by the response – I thought all primary schools made a fuss of Mother's Day, churning out paper bouquets and cards with pictures of kittens on them like they were going out of fashion – I went away reassured that I had the event covered.

However, the Friday before Mothering Sunday my daughter came back from school looking very subdued and so I asked her what was wrong. She said that her class had been to a 'special' assembly where the deputy head had waxed lyrical about how wonderful mothers are and how the children should take really good care of them. 'OK,' I said, not quite sure what to say. 'So, how was that?' 'It was really embarrassing,' she replied sadly. 'All my friends kept turning round and looking at me and asking if I was alright, but I didn't want them to,' she explained.

Thanks, Miss Whatever-Your-Name-Was of Class 5!

Yes, I know schools are busy places and there is always lots going on, but I would have thought it possible for my daughter not to have been put in that position. What can you do at your school and across your curriculum to deal with such situations with a little more tact and understanding? Are you vigilant on Mother's Day, Father's Day, anniversaries and birthdays for children who may be that little bit more fragile on such days? The last thing we are suggesting is that you don't bother with such events (or rename them 'Surviving Carer's Day') or even exclude the grieving child from them. Just give them warning. Show you are thinking. Show the child – and the parent – you care.

And it is not just annual events like these to watch out for – dealing with life after death in the RE curriculum or with illnesses in areas such as biology or with tales of loss in English. All of these can be approached with sensitivity but not soppiness. In my son's college, before a lesson that was going to touch on issues to do with mental illness, his tutor discreetly took him to one side and explained what the topic was going to be. She gave my son the choice of not attending or sitting there without joining in or of joining in as he saw fit. She made it clear that if at any point he felt he needed to leave then that would be fine. No questions asked. What she did, apart from taking away that awful element of surprise that the grieving person has to deal with on a daily basis, was to give him choice. And at a time in a young person's life when they feel there is so much that is out of their control, with all the concomitant levels of stress such a situation generates, she had given the reins to his life back to him. Wonderful!

My son then went into the lesson and joined in with some of his own experiences in a mature, balanced and un-mawkish way.

Honestly, it is not that hard.

TWELVE

When another parent dies, make sure you are mindful of other children who have lost parents, or indeed any loved one, as it will bring many memories back.

As we have already heard, around 41,000 children a year have to come to terms with losing a parent. That is one bereaved child every twenty-two minutes who will be desperate for the help and support of the professionals in his or her young life.

Add that to the Childhood Bereavement Network's statistics that 3,000 young people each year die as a result of accidents or serious illness, that seventeen babies a day will die at or soon after birth and that 6,000 families a year are affected by suicide, and you know that sooner or later, probably sooner, you will have to deal with a child at your school dealing with such an issue. And then it will happen again, to another child.

If you have acknowledged the various suggestions from our own experiences in this book, as well as made use of the training and resources offered by the organisations listed in the resources section, then well done. However, apart from mobilising yourself for the newly bereaved child you also need to look over your shoulder at the recently bereaved.

In my middle child's school, within a few months of my wife's death another mother died, and in similar circumstances. How the school handled the particular girl who was in my daughter's year I do not know. She had also lost her father several years before and I think she ended up in care. While I would want the school to do everything it could to support the bereaved child, it would have been helpful for someone, maybe the class tutor or the head of year, to have had a quiet, discreet word with my daughter to see how she was too.

Again, I know that schools are busy places and that, as institutions, they do tend to have short memories. Life goes on relentlessly and SATs, exams, parents' evenings and training days come and go like the passing of the seasons. Yet, if you want to show that being a caring school is more than just a motto for your prospectus between 'putting people first' and 'bringing out the best in every child', then these are the areas in which you have to prove your mettle.

THIRTEEN

Learn about helping children to cope with bereavement from the various agencies out there.

This book is just a personal view from first-hand experience about what schools can do – and should not do – to help a grieving child. But it is just one tool in a whole arsenal of support available to all professionals who are in the position, whether they like it or not, of supporting a young person through the worst time of their life.

From what I have seen there is no expectation that there should be a whole-school policy on supporting a grieving child, and training seems to be down to the individual rather than something that is addressed by institutions. However, sending someone on a course offered by the sorts of organisations listed in the resources section of this book, buying a few resources and maybe having the teacher not so much 'cascade' what they have learned as 'distil' it into a few key points that are easy to grasp, easy to find among all the other school bumph when you need to (and, as we saw in the previous lesson, you *will* need to) and easy to perform, would be a half-day's training very well spent.

Remember, of course, that among your staff there will be those who are also recently bereaved or who perhaps also lost a parent when they were at school. The same rules apply to them as apply to the child in Lesson Eleven. If the situation is handled sensitively they will have a great deal to offer their colleagues in this element of their professional development.

The majority of these organisations offer support packs and resources as well as providing training for the whole school or for a nominated individual. Winston's Wish, named after the Winston Churchill Fellowship that founder and clinical psychologist Julie Stokes, OBE was granted to study childhood bereavement in the United States and Canada in the early 1990s, has even teamed up with Teachers TV for a video showing how professionals from their organisations helped children from a primary school and a secondary school come to terms with their respective losses.

There may well be other, more local support on offer too. We were living in Suffolk when my wife died and, through the Family Carers support we were receiving anyway, we were put in contact with a local hospice, St Nicholas in Bury St Edmunds. They ran a bereavement support group specifically for children called Nicky's Way, and in the months following our loss all three of my children benefited from spending time with Yvonne (who wrote the foreword to the original book) who supported them in a professional, effective and knowledgeable way. It is because of this support – entirely free to us – that all proceeds from the original book went to Nicky's Way.

One simple procedure you can put in place immediately is to nominate a room, near reception, that can be used to break bad news to a child. In my daughter's infant school the head teacher was away so we were ushered into her office while the secretary went to find my daughter. It was a small school so it was a process that did not take very long. In my elder daughter's secondary school, however, I had to ask for a room we could use, which turned out to be the head of year's office – several twisty, endless corridors from the main reception area where my daughter had been brought to me. That was a long, long, hurried walk, leading my daughter by the hand as she followed in agitated silence, fearing the worst. Yet I know that the school had various rooms and offices behind the main reception area that would have served the purpose just as well.

When the ashen-faced parent turns up in your reception and asks for their son or daughter to be brought out of class to tell them the news, what will your procedure be to make that awful event slightly less traumatic and problematic for those concerned?

Whether you look to local support offered by a hospice or church group, to the large national organisations such as Winston's Wish or Cruse, or even international ones such as Rainbows, be assured that you will be learning invaluable insights and approaches. You may not know when they will be called upon but you can be certain that day will come in some shape or form. Then you will know that it was time and money well spent.

FOURTEEN

Time heals in bereavement as much as it does following an amputation. It is just what you go through to come to terms with things better.

Time, they say in bereavement, as with many of life's traumas, heals. But healing implies getting better, going back to how it was, being as good as before. In bereavement this is not the case. It never goes back to how it was before. It never goes away. Life gets better, not because of the absence of the pain but because you learn to live your life despite it.

One woman my girls and I met at the conference I mentioned on page 8 suggested that we see grieving like a 'pebble in your pocket'. It is always there. It is uncomfortable at times. It sticks into you when you least expect it. But at times you can get it out and hold it, look at it, deal with it in your hands. And it is painful and distressing but at least it is real and tangible and concrete, and you want to cry and you do cry, but then you can put the pebble back in your pocket, until the next time, and get on with your life.

My wife's brother died in an accident when he was nineteen. Being on the edge of a distraught family in this way showed me that what grieving individuals want most is to talk about the person who has died. And that does not go away with time. My wife still suffered terribly on the anniversary of her younger brother's death and also on his birthdays. I have since seen this with other people I have met who have been bereaved. I talk to them about the person they have lost and, without fail, they thank me for it. Why? Because everyone else skirts round the subject and would rather talk about the weather than the person who has died, would even rather cross the road than talk about that person. Remember, just because the person is not weeping inconsolably does not mean they have forgotten or that time has 'healed' them. It simply means they are not weeping inconsolably at that moment. They will again. Then they'll stop again. That is the way it goes. So, if you are worried about talking to someone about their loss for fear of upsetting them, don't worry. They are upset anyway, just hiding it. And talking to them will help. Why? Because talking about the person is the only thing that keeps that person alive, that's why.

As I mentioned in Lesson Four, both of my daughters have been approached by young children who take them through the same sort of childish logic:

Child: Is it true your mum has died?

My daughters: Yes.

Child: I think you're lying.

My daughters: No, it's true.

Child: Well, why aren't you crying then?

My daughters: It doesn't work like that. Now go away ...

So, when it comes to supporting the grieving child in your class or in your care, keep at it. Be there for them for the long haul. Show them you care by remembering to show them you care on an ongoing basis. Remembering is so important to them now. It is all they've got of the person they've lost. Do your bit.

FIFTEEN

And thank you for taking the time to read this. You can make a terrible situation a bit less stressful for a grieving family.

I'm sorry if I have come across as a little blunt in some of my views over the course of this book. I guess seeing your children being unnecessarily upset at a time when you need all the support you can get to help them can make you rather grumpy.

For those of you who have read this far, though, may I – may we – thank you for taking the time to do so. Nothing can take away the pain of the loss the children are dealing with. But your actions – little ones, whole-school ones, genuine ones, professional ones, personal ones – can and will make an awful scenario just that little bit easier to deal with. And in doing so you will help the parent know that, when his or her children go back to school in the days or weeks after the tragic day, they will be cared for and supported in a way that actually counts, and allows the whole family to start the process of picking up the shattered pieces of their lives and moving on.

And for that we thank you.

VII

RESOURCES

Royalties from this book will go to leading UK children's bereavement charity Winston's Wish, with which Independent Thinking has recently been collaborating:

www.winstonswish.org

Do especially check out the Thunks on Death we have put together for their website to encourage schools to start conversations around death, loss and grieving:

www.winstonswish.org/wp-content/uploads/2019/06/Winstons-Wish-thunks.pdf

The following charities and organisations are also doing important work in this area and there may well be support local to you to help too:

www.childbereavementuk.org

Child Bereavement UK's free online resources for schools might be of particular interest:

https://www.childbereavementuk.org/online-learning-for-schools

www.childhoodbereavementnetwork.org.uk

www.childline.org.uk

www.cruse.org.uk

www.griefencounter.org.uk/young-people

www.hopeagain.org.uk

www.rainbows.org

https://stnicholashospice.org.uk/support-and-information/getting-help/counselling-and-emotional-support/living-with-bereavement/nickys-way-support-for-children

Good luck.

LESLEY

1964–2008

At peace

independent thinking

Independent Thinking. An education company.

Taking people's brains for a walk since 1994.

We use our words.

www.independentthinking.com